CENTS POEMS

CENTS POEMS

SYNTYCHE AKABLAN

Parents

Siblings

"The BIG Small Group"

"One Scrub"

Friends

With all my heart.

CONTENTS

Notes

PART I

None is expected to understand the poems.

Labyrinths, mazes they are.

Unknown,

Now and maybe Forever.

Do not let Them fool ye.

1. Introspection Tears

(02. January 2023)

Tears to catch the face
Flowing in a slower pace
To mimic the past fades
To be forgotten about
But before, doubts have to be settled

2. What do you want from me?

(02. January 2023)

They are after what cannot be obtained
Impossible — that makes it possible — to believe
Magical how beautiful such an illusion is
The canvasses of the ideal are delicately painted
Impossible that makes it possible to believe

3. Vice City

(11. January 2023)

A shred of joy and hope is food for the poor
At their table
The "uppers" think they are on the top floor
A power that is not that stable
Countless times, the same fable

4. Ticking clock

(02. April 2023)

We were given time
They said that we could create
See that you can be lost in your creation
Who is the fool now!

5. Mask on or off

(02. April 2023)

Precious people
Such a warm thing
To feel
To fear
That insanity is coupled

6. Vintage Toxicity

(02. April 2023)

is it desire or hate
in your eyes
it doesn't matter
as long as on
me, your eyes
is it water
flowing down your cheeks
i feel submerged
are you tearing
love, joy, anger **or** disgust
why don't you choose

7. To love is hard

(06. April 2023)

I don't know what you want
But I (will) try my best to give you all
So don't make me fool
So don't make me fall
Fall in love
Fall for love
Under your world

8. Gone, but still

(15. April 2023)

She left you only with her warm hands
that wrote what she used to defend
Now, she is cold
Without the sky,
She blew through your ears
So that you could feel the fresh atmosphere
That she promoted, on your heads.
Some outside forces, she defeated barehanded, bare head

9. Tree

(16. April 2023)

The petals as the red carpet
For them to walk graciously
Losing my flowers, my shine for you..

10. Unconsumable Spirit

(16. April 2023)

From the snap of the fingers
Snatch the soul-eating desire
It's time for such a devouring enemy
To leave the heart, heart on fire
Filled with luscious swindlers

11. What am I if not who I am

(22. April 2023)

I am not fire.
I am type-water.
I flow immensely
To wash away or bring in
Then, I can stagnate abruptly
To let in or out.

12. Butter'fuckinflies

(25. April 2023)

Got them Butter'fuckinflies
No clue about how to make them fly
Away from the words stacked in my throat
Stuck in my head, my mind still has a coat
Losing me to the Butter'fuckinflies

13. Ghost Kermis

(01. May 2023)

Unhappy or happy is the look
The ghosts fading as sailed is the boat
The wind blows harder than usual
There is hope, a rope[1]
To swing on the attractions while holding tight

14. Freedom

(04. May 2023)

You all keep saying that Happiness is free
I paid for mine though
Did you lie
Or does free mean cheap
As one's expense is not always expensive

15. Under Cover

(14. May 2023)

There is not just one page in a book
If one wants to see from a judgemental look
One should appreciate the pages a bit closer
The stories could be different from the cover

16. when there is no one else

(16. May 2023)

The times when I felt lost
A wave left by the coast
I was before my **own** world, the host
Keeping me hostage
Far from the stage
My **own** fault, my mind is an immense cage

17. nobody wants you

(21. May 2023)

You are too perfect
You have too many imperfections
Nobody wants you
Only you should rip your all for their commotion
Your neutrality is more like a zero
Also an antagonist, you're **not** more than a hero

18. Seea

(21. May 2023)

What's in you that I can't see
Fires in the sky
Skyrocketing, gaining height
When are we going to navigate on board of sea

19. Backpain

(31. May 2023)

Sue me
Harder than the sun on my skin
Shout me
Harder than the pain of the after-me, after-keen

20. One end meets another

(03. June 2023)

The clear ways to the pattern
The privilege is not always given
Then turning a round
Earth with extremities that you keep round
For all to meet again
Whether or not it was allowed

21. Motionless

(03. June 2023)

Eyes burning **from** desire and lust
All red even though they seem at rest
Close them for real peace
Hoping the nightmares won't ace

22. Payday

(05. June 2023)

We laugh until it's not funny
We run even after the finish line

23

(06. June 2023)

Many more
Maybe more
Do all (?) make me someone I do not know

24. Sour Beverage

(09. June 2023)

Shots of desire to drink
Heavy taste to feel down the throat
Love is dimmed, it is a shrink
A block of ice – these strangling feelings, these threats

25. Shiny us

(10. June 2023)

Is there enough space in space for us
Us-like, Is the universe strong and sure to trust
Are we made of void, empty hearts and empty minds
Were we praying so that each other we could find
Us, The glitters in the sky, in my soul
Love sounds blind

26. Soft Rock

(11. June 2023)

A soft rock that I am
Will you expose me at the centre of your attention

27. Headaches

(12. June 2023)

The free spirit condensed in one mind
The new Us say(s) Love, but don't do it
The world in which the I still can't find a fit
The I opens the blinds for the thoughts at wind

28. Hunger for hatred

(16. June 2023)

Tell me that I am not good enough
I crave sadness
Then I can write about it and all the madness

29. Sight

(18. June 2023)

When you do not show me love
Why should I look in your direction
If love is not what I will see
Harvest of the seeds

30. O Lord, I am trying

(18. June 2023)

«Oh hi, I just wanted to hi you”
It's what to give when you miss them
After, the previous theme

31. Cannot change anyone

(24. June 2023)

Only time changes the world
People's perspectives can be shaped
You either broaden or tighten them
It means, educating or **misteaching**

32. Promisses

(24. June 2023)

Until death do us part
Why don't you leave me
Piece after piece, you are tearing me apart
Why don't you leave my being

33. Fill it in.

(24. June 2023)

Lost in my body
My soul does not seem to find its self in me
Anymore
Many tries to find my self in vivo
I feel like having nothing to lose
No more

34. Perception

(24. June 2023)

Too precious, too cute, too fragile
These're what's stopping me from hurting you
The tough emotions that I cannot share on your mind
You cannot hear us, your Love is not audile

35. Pain

(02. July 2023)

Locked away
From one source of well-being
Nothing is enough to find a way
The maze, I let myself in

36. Néant

(04. July 2023)

Pile of dreams
Condensed, like angels on monsters
My free choice is endangered

37. Passionate Crime

(06. July 2023)

I am not a murderer
The will to kill everything bearing your scent
Is consuming the inside me
Might thus take my **own** life
My memory, the carrier of them like paint stains

38. The love consistency gives

(04. July 2023)

With passion comes satisfaction
Accomplishment of fascinating things
Greatest is made by fractions
On my skin, the feel of tears made of thrills

39. Home again

(11. July 2023)

My heart is heavy from the emotions that it has been storing
Can you rock it so that it feels at home again
Let me let go of everything so I won't feel the pain
In your arms, my freedom I abandon

40. Cosmic

(11. July 2023)

Every time I swim in your eyes
Full of our **made-up** galaxy
The one I forced myself to see
Every time I swim (swam) in your eyes

41. kNew HEiR

(15. July 2023)

It has started again
Feels quick — such a game
Escapism from the drama to face
It had started again
Before the *latter* stopped
Toes escalate the ladder with a new pace

42. New words

(16. July 2023)

I declined the rhyming offers
This is all only anodyne
Not that I am irascible
However, the ruling surrounding poetry feels canard
My written sentences show off intense pusillanimity
The one who reads me is disgruntled

43. Stalemate

(17. July 2023)

My feelings got locked
They couldn't move anymore
The bars got me in Stalemate
In a draw for a conclusion
Where none would win

44. Silence

(20. July 2023)

I have lost some words
In a way similar to the trees with their leaves
Seasonal fever, beating the drums of my world
Did I talk too much already?
This is too much to heave

45. Bear with me, please

(20. July 2023)

Afraid to write **for** you
As you can disappear anytime
Did not know, I would fall for you
Also, might my love not be light
A lot to handle,
I will hunt your thoughts like a crime and a chime

46. Still

(30. July 2023)

In need of it
That is what is wanted by the absence
My senses in a euphoric state
Privileging the hot air balloon
Head in the clouds
Refreshing scents scrambled to lift my moon

47. Writing up

(30. July 2023)

The new level is unlocked
The new label inked into the soul
Only Miracle can deliver us from the past matching tattoo
Only Miracle can deliver us from this new matching tattoo
Which level did one achieve

48. Foul

(07. August 2023)

Powerful or Power-fools
Crazy for control, if available
Changing ways, if there is no tool
Trials that do not give outcomes for us to be stable
How much of you did you bring to the table

49. Leak

(08. August 2023)

A broken heart, even
When reconstituted, will not be fair anymore
Leak of emotions from the open sides

50. What's left

(10. August 2023)

The first part is never the easiest step
What's left of your thoughts on me
Travelling through $\frac{1}{50}$ of my mind[2]
These 50 Cents Poems or 50 Cents Texts
Wait.
What's the real value of anything.?

PART II

Welcome to the last fifty of the hundred.

Part I and II might have nothing in common, but it is good to see where *Cents Poems* started (cf. Part I).

An ending usually does not taste pleasant without acknowledgement of the start.

51. is also related to the eyes as they are a mirror to see our inside world.

Windows to the outside world, glass-doors...

51. SSD

(01. November 2023)

Eyes are the clouds of the sky
Bad weather, nice weather
Or just some feelings in the middle
Open cosmos but still a riddle
The windows to the soul or outside theatre
After witnessing, it is in, somewhere in your sky

52. Trading

(01. November 2023)

As soon as the universe hears us crying
We all start to trade
Our tears for a moment of joy
We give a part of us during our lifetime

53. Curator

(19. November 2023)

We are looking for the cure
Might be to kill the curse
Fallen Apple,
Bitten Fruit,
Forbidd(/tt)en one,
Or just xes.

54. Truth or Dare

(19. November 2023)

The truth is in between the right ∩* the left
I am in the middle of U
In truth
I am on U
In truth
Dare me to balance on this slim path
If I do not fail not to fall
For U

*and

55. Cease-Fire

(03. December 2023)

Be the water to my fire
Or let us do it the other way around
Burns from you that I ease
With the water, I cannot not
Drink
Even if hard to stir
Courage that I lease
For the inside can, because there itself couldn't be found

56. The Coup

(19. December 2023)

Love at first sight
I had a second one too - another sight
Despite the cease-fire
Against my flammable loneliness
Loathe, fore-sigh

57. Significant Figures

(22. December 2023)

Adding you as a plus to my life
Nothing changes
You're the zero to the addition
You're the zero to the multiplication
I am still one after you

58. Handwriting

(22. December 2023)

They made me do it
Who made you do it
Brain and Heart
They wanted to try it

it:
To exchange their respective roles

59. Overtime

(04. January 2024)

Ruminating might be what over-thinkers
Do
You contemplate the beauty of
Your mistakes
?

60. Quoting

(07. January 2024)

Do not fire me
If you do not intend to later match my energy
Some use dreams to get back
And make you live a dream

61. Outdoors

(11. January 2024)

Uniforms that I do not wear
I am an outsider
My faces that I cannot see
Elsewhere
I am an outsider

62. In-App Purchases

(11. January 2024)

My character has not yet
Unlocked some features
I still cannot close my eyes
As the colour behind them
Is not light

63. Make it Your Own

(17. January 2024)

Honours
Senior
Hall
Devotion
Hail
Call
Intuition
Nail

64. My Own

(17. January 2024)

I felt the call
In my ear, and out to the hall
They were giving me honours
Pressing on the ice-cold hail
With the "it's alright" fingernail
Slow feet-prints for some devotion
I felt that "being a senior"
After you stepped by intuition

65. Snowy x In Love

(20. x 21. January 2024)

Walking on eggshells
One tries not to fall
When on the glossy tales full of surprises
And on the in-love-to-fall ways
There is: the humming of the valves sways

66. Lies x Fears

(21. January 2024)

Fear lies within what cannot be controlled
Lie fears missing a part, tone of veracity
Fears lie that they will not be uncovered
Lies fear the after-truth x self-pity

67. Dans Les Bois

(26. January 2024)

Running to whomever is behind
All of this that I cannot yet see
The friction from the layers
I run through, are slowing me down
All of this that I can then see
Is exactly the sucking mud

68. Appetite

(21. February 2024)

No thought runs in my head
Although I am still suffocating in them
I am not that one anymore
This part has got lost as time runs
How is **I** going to catch up

69. Willy

(23. February 2024)

I am willing to listen
To my voice only
At least deliberately
So that I could grab the pen
And write the ends
So that I could make the world
Better ends
After all,
I am willing to listen
To the voices of you around

70. Drive Way

(23. February 2024)

The drive needed
To ride the circular
That I need to start the engine
To set the pedal on fire
For the gas to consume each tire

71. Seventy-one

(DD.MM.YYYY)

72. Seventy-two

(DD.MM.YYYY)

73. Frod

(24. February 2024)

Que? Still looking for N°71 & 72?
Allow me to You.
Allow me to Me.
The blank spaces are what I feel
Sometimes in my mind
If You felt scammed
That's how I feel when there is nothing
Moving through Me.
The essence that helps Me
Forget that I could be a Frod

74. The Runs Storpt

(04. March 2024)

I wish to have a walk
With my sanity only
With you only
A walk to breathe out the runs
In the trees,
Where no irrationality finds itself

75. Truth or Care

(29. Feb 2024)

Out loud the truth
Or do we care
For them not to be hurt
Not by the sword of the words,
But by the pace, each&every letter scratches
The (now) confused heart
Out loud the truth
If we do dare

76. A fix is what we all need..

(07. March 2024)

As harsh as it might sound
The world is the first hell
It is just an "entrée" for the sinners
Humanity-ties
And lies
Without humanity
i.e., human nature playing ties
With the worst

77. Asymptotes, The Re-edition

(07. March 2024)

We can say that Love Is
Love is a parallel universe
With us, the asymptotes
We always tend to, but never achieve
We keep trying, but not to conclude

78. Fever Dream

(07. March 2024)

Set me on **fye**
It's okay, I am Water
The breeze of your ignition
Could light me up
All day
Long or Short
Drown me underwater
It's okay, I am Light
For your shine to be by my power

79. Weather

(12. March 2024)

Your voice gave me shivers
Now, I wish that you could see these verses
Well written together, not like us
Fate betrayed our trust

80. Lost Queswers

(27. March 2024)

Confused,
We have many questions
Out of curiosity,
We make up many answers
Some of them (even) without questions
These are **Queswers**
Also Quest for Answers
When we have them continually
These are Lost **Queswers**

81. Travel

(28. March 2024)

There is this tendency of estimating
The values of others as more
Astronomical, only when within
There is no thing
There is this lore that no one knows:
There is enough for all

82. Bizarre

(28. March 2024)

I wish I could draw a break
With diverse emotions from my heart
On the paper, making it a wallpaper
An old sensation of being **for** here
But also still for there
Breaking free
Abusing the strokes of the pastels

83. Breathtaking Journey

(30. March 2024)

Dying is reviving but somewhere new
Happy for another side are only a few
Am somewhat a few, it is part of the journey
Losing breath to gain **(for)** some time, attention
Maturing into a piece of mind, souvenir

84. Lyric, -ism

(30. March 2024)

I will write about myself
And other selves,
For everyone to have the illusion of
Understanding me as a person
And other selves,
As a person or many selves.

85. Wintrees

(14. April 2024)

Until the ideal is found
The wolf will remain a loner

The End.

86. Asterism

(14. April 2024)

You can still see the sky from afar
Whether it's falling
or Getting away from your radar.
Scan the sand.
Can you see its sky?
Each has one[3]
With diverse stars.

87. Elephant in the Rhum

(17. April 2024)

The issue is bigger than the size fitting your look
Handling some glasses to resize it or making it disappear
To be handled with care for nothing to be poured all over
All over the Rhum
Afterwards, the memory monster resurfaces

88. Furnace

(19. April 2024)

O to be!
where the heat makes one lose senses
where death is not at ease
where depth is also not
Before the furnace, being part of the previous world
To make sense

89. Nano

(19. April 2024)

I did not walk to arrive,
i scrolled
through the mind's number-one magazines
Finger-skating is what it could have looked like
One particular story is a bestseller
I keep buying[4] it.

90. Seasonal

(04. May 2024)

I taste the spring
In my mind, always that bud
That keeps growing only when Springs
The new, also old as it keeps
Bouncing
Making my heart run miles

91. Goodbyes x Brand New

(02. May 2024 x 16. May 2024)

A whistle of sunny something-that-is-inexplicable[5]
Sunny
Is exactly how it feels
Funny
Is actually how it thrills
My skin, and hampers my heartbeats
Delightful are all bits (beats)

92. Right!

(11. May 2024)

Hey, you!
Do it right!
What exactly are those expectations that I cannot
Fulfil
What is "it"?
What exactly are those emotions that I cannot
Fully Feel
Don't shout at me!
My mind has sensitive ears!
I told them out loud.

93. Above the Fence

(15. May 2024)

More substance for substantive existence
To replay the debris of that absence
To be enchanted again and again
after each round
Regardless of not being around
For that stance to dwell

94. Critics

(17. May 2024)

What is going to happen when
The spark dies
When blank are those files
Would the murmurs like the honours
Of executing the tens out of ten

95. Limited

(18. May 2024)

A limited edition of a mind is a saturated
Mind that (anymore) does not mind
There is no space to set anything in
There is also no way of letting go
Of previous add-ins that had sunk in

96. Guest

(18. May 2024)

My soul is likely not a guest around you
But in its home, around itself and I
And I, should ask for permission to enter its abode too
After wandering around for myself

97. Time flies

(18. May 2024)

Time flies, but where is it going
Pursuing happiness or
Hurrying the disaster
Soon will tell us what happened before we joined
Pursuing happiness or
Hurrying the disaster
Later will make us wish we had done differently

98. Almost There

(19. May 2024)

Crossing the nonchalant bridge
It appears so!
Is it though?!
Made of tiles that will shine and ring...
Once a step on them
To make you inspire that melody of life

99. Summary

(19. May 2024)

The sum of all texts li(v)es within each of them
I went through Tears.
Left at high miles per hour for a Hundred Books
That could be a pace too brisk for them
But not for me when
At a certain life interval, everything seemed Motionless
A Travel similar to Fever Dreams that never stop running
Always wondering if the process is over the timing
Always wondering when to start ruining

100. It's not a 1000

(19. April 2024)

We are likely last in someone's life development
Likely non-existent in their epilogue
What about ours?
What about yours?
Are you still there?
Writing the 100?

It will all come out great.
Do not trust the process, but you.

III BONUS

Here are three additional poems because delight was felt while writing *Cents Poems*.

These poems could hopefully also be considered substitutes for 71 and 72.

Enjoy them.

101. The Rhythm of Silence

(08. March 2024)

The rhythm of silence bounces in my head
I always need somewhere to disappear,
to leave
An unknown place where to live
In the safe and sound, with nothing
else to hear
But the rhythm of silence
Somewhere with no suspense

102. Fragile

(25. March 2024)

A label is what to run away from.
The world where I am from
Could stick one or too many on you
Then you must stick to A Label
Bear the heavy on your shoulder
Otherwise, you are A Fragile Label

103. However

(15.&27. March 2024)

Despite us, the nights keep insisting on
How hard it is to live/leave a-part
Plus, minds wander to wonder on
The never-well-made story of us
Despite us, the days shine more than
The sparks in your irides

1.   The rope of a "swing" whose equivalent is "balançoire" in French.
   The purpose is to have fun and let the **Bad** swings out of one's mind.

2.   1/50 is Part 1 which is 50 Poems or the 50 Poems of Part 1 are 50/100 so 1/2.
    2/100 is Part 2 making the 100 poems ("*Cents Poems*") or both parts that make the "100 poems", one book.

3.   "We all have one sky." could replace this line.

4.   Set the link between "story" and the last verse.

5.   Ineffable feeling.

www.ingramcontent.com/pod-product-compliance
Lightning Source LLC
LaVergne TN
LVHW031243190726
843493LV00010B/2993